Teen Survival Guides

Developing Social Awareness

JENNIFER SANDERSON

CHERITON
CHILDREN'S BOOKS

Published in 2026 by **Cheriton Children's Books**
1 Bank Drive West, Shrewsbury, Shropshire, SY3 9DJ, UK

First Edition

Author: Jennifer Sanderson
Designer: Paul Myerscough
Editor: Kelly Short
Proofreader: Amy Strauss

Picture credits: Cover: Shutterstock/Halay Alex. Inside: p4: Shutterstock/SeventyFour, p5: Shutterstock/Pics Five, p6: Shutterstock/Jose Calsina, p7: Shutterstock/Emma Manners, p8: Shutterstock/Diego Cervo, p9: Shutterstock/Motortion Films, p11: Shutterstock/Ground Picture, p13: Shutterstock/Alejandro J. Vivas, p14: Shutterstock/Evrymmnt, p15: Shutterstock/Monkey Business Images, p16: Shutterstock/Creatista, p17: Shutterstock/Jihan Nafiaa Zahri, p19: Shutterstock/Motortion Films, p20: Shutterstock/Fizkes, p21: Shutterstock/Monkey Business Images, p22: Shutterstock/MJTH, p23: Shutterstock/Jacob Lund, p24: Shutterstock/Perfect Wave, p27: Shutterstock/XArtProduction, p28: Shutterstock/Halfpoint, p29: Shutterstock/VH Studio, p30: Shutterstock/Fizkes, p31: Shutterstock/LightField Studios, p32: Shutterstock/Jacob Lund, p33: Shutterstock/Monkey Business Images, p34: Shutterstock/Carlos Caetano, p35: Shutterstock/Krakenimages.com, p37: Shutterstock/Monkey Business Images, p38: Shutterstock/PeopleImages.com/Yuri A, p39: Shutterstock/SynthEx, p41: Shutterstock, p42: Shutterstock/Monkey Business Images, p43: Shutterstock/Ground Picture, p44: Shutterstock/Maria Sbytova, p45: Shutterstock/Lopolo, p46: Shutterstock/Inna Reznik, p47: Shutterstock/Mooremedia, p49: Shutterstock/SynthEx, p50: Shutterstock/Vasara, p51: Shutterstock/Tijana Simic, p52: Shutterstock/Xavier Lorenzo, p53: Shutterstock/Shisu Ka, p54: Shutterstock/DimaBerlin, p55: Shutterstock/Shakirov Albert, p57: Shutterstock/BalanceFormCreative, p58: Shutterstock/Ground Picture, p59: Shutterstock/BAZA Production.

Printed in China

Contents

INTRODUCTION

Reading the Room

You've probably heard it before, but being a teenager is tough. That's because you are going through a lot of changes, all at once. Physical and mental adjustments are happening because of the hormonal changes that come with puberty. But what people don't always tell you is that your world is changing too. When you were younger, your family was your world. But now, as you're growing up and becoming independent, your world is getting a lot bigger.

STUDIES IN TEEN SURVIVAL

A lot of change takes place during your teenage years. Along with physical, mental, and emotional changes, teenagers are also trying to figure out their identities, what they believe in, and what their values are. Teenagers also want to be independent of their parents. They feel the need to spend more time away from them, often with their friends and peers. Working on social-awareness skills makes this transition, or change, easier.

Your World Is Widening

As a teenager, you'll find yourself among peers at school who are suddenly very important to you. Later, you'll work with colleagues, and will likely spend more time with them than you do with your family. You are becoming part of a wider world, and you need to find your space within it. How you fit in to the wider world and how you can contribute to it will help you live a fulfilled and happy life. One way to do this is by being socially aware.

As you grow up, your world changes and your friends become increasingly important to you.

Conflict is a natural part of life but it's important to learn the skills to resolve it as smoothly as possible.

Skills for Life

Being socially aware means that you're able to respond to social situations appropriately. Some people call it being able to "read the room." Like most things in life, social awareness doesn't just happen overnight. It takes practice and includes mastering, or at least trying to master, several skills. In this book, we'll look at ten social-awareness skills that are important to learn now, while you're a teenager. If you can get a handle on them at this stage of your life, it will make being an adult much easier. These skills are:

- **Emotional awareness**
- **Considering perspectives**
- **Cooperation**
- **Effective communication**
- **Reading social cues**
- **Identifying strengths and weaknesses in others**
- **Kindness**
- **Conflict resolution**
- **Diversity awareness**
- **Giving back**

We'll explain what these terms mean as we work through the book and explore them in workshops. By the time you've finished the book, you'll understand what they mean. Even better, you'll have learned some important social-awareness skills—skills you can use for the rest of your life.

CHAPTER 1

It's an Emotional Time

Emotions are feelings. They tell us what we're experiencing and they help us react to a situation. Everyone feels emotions—they're part of being human. For example, babies smile or laugh when they are happy, and they cry (sometimes a lot!) when they are unhappy. When children grow up, they learn more about emotions and what certain emotions feel like. As a teenager, you are learning to label the emotions you experience.

Hormones: They're Everywhere!

From the age of around seven or eight, your body starts to produce the hormones that cause growth and other physical changes. At the same time, hormones are also responsible for the mood swings that teenagers go through. You may be happy, sad, and everything in between—all in one day. It's no wonder people often say that teenagers' emotions are all over the place.

Being a teenager can feel exhausting: One minute you're really happy but then, suddenly, something can upset you.

You Can't Stop Them

The good news is that your friends and peers are probably going through the same hormonal changes that you are. Look around you and you'll soon see that you aren't the only one with zits, if you have them. The bad news is that you can't stop hormonal changes and the emotional roller coaster that comes with those big changes.

It's fine to feel a certain way, whether it's positive or negative, but you need to learn to be aware of your emotions.

Embrace the Change

Being a teenager means you need to learn to embrace the changes and emotional turmoil this stage of your life brings. It's helpful to remember that emotions come and go. Most are fleeting feelings that pass. Some emotions are positive, and you'll feel happy, loving, confident, inspired, and cheerful. Others are more negative. You may be angry, resentful, afraid, ashamed, guilty, or low and sad. Sometimes, emotions can linger to become a mood, and whether that's a good or bad mood, it's OK. It's important to remember that there is no right or wrong emotion. Every emotion you feel is valid.

Teen Need to Know

Sometimes, teenagers feel things that they can't explain or that they think no one will understand. Instead of trying to talk about this, they may keep their emotions to themselves. This can lead to much bigger problems and emotional distress. Teenagers experiencing distress may show signs of depression. That can include sadness, trouble sleeping, lack of energy, and substance use and abuse. They may also be anxious. Signs of anxiety include excessive irritability, difficulty with concentrating and sleeping, headaches, and fatigue.

Let's Talk about Emotional Awareness

Each day you experience hundreds of different emotions. You may think of something and it makes you laugh or feel good about yourself. Or perhaps, something makes you feel sad or anxious. Next time you feel something, try to stop and think for a moment. Can you name the emotion that you are feeling? Labeling your emotions is a skill that helps you understand them. If you can label how something makes you feel, you'll be able to use this skill to understand yourself better or act on emotions. For example, if you feel sad when a friend says hurtful things, you'll realize that you don't want a friend who does that, but would rather be friends with someone who is kinder and makes you feel good. Either way, labeling your emotions is key to being emotionally aware.

When you can label an emotion, you will be more empathetic. This means you will be able to understand another person's emotions.

Defining Social-Awareness Skills: Emotional Awareness

Emotional awareness means recognizing, respecting, and accepting your feelings as they happen. When you are aware of your own emotions, you'll be able to recognize and respect other people's emotions too. Being emotionally aware means taking a deep breath before you react to your own or someone else's emotions. If you are not emotionally aware, you won't make good decisions. As a result, your relationships may suffer, and you'll have difficulty understanding others.

THE SOCIAL-AWARENESS WORKSHOP

Not Reading the Room

Problems can crop up when you don't develop emotional awareness. Take a look at this scenario: Imagine you and your friend both do well in science. You often study together before a big test. When your teacher tells you about a prize for the student who scores the highest in your next test, you both want to win.

You both work hard for the test, but it is tough. Your friend scores 2 percent higher than you. You are disappointed that you didn't win. In fact, you feel angry. But you also feel confused about your feelings. You don't want to see your friend, and don't want to study with them again. You go home without speaking to them. You stay in your room for the rest of the night, and don't return your friend's messages.

THE SOCIAL-AWARENESS WORKSHOP

Same situation, but with emotional awareness.

Recognizing Emotions

When your teacher tells you and your friend about a prize for the student who scores the highest mark in your next test, you both want to win. You work hard for the test, but it is pretty tough.

Your friend scores 2 percent higher than you. You are disappointed, angry, and confused. At home, you tell your mom what has happened. She helps you figure out why you feel upset. She also helps you decide what to say to your friend, and encourages you to speak to them. You go to your friend's house and explain how you feel. You talk it out. They say they understand how you feel, and say next time you'll win for sure.

What Works Better Here?:

- You acknowledge your feelings, and that they are confusing.
- You speak to your mom about how you feel.
- You then talk with your friend, and explain how you are feeling.
- Sharing your feelings helps you figure them out and feel better.

Being Emotionally Aware—What Can It Do for You?

When you have difficult emotions, talking to someone you trust can help you label them and work through them. Being aware of others' emotions too will help you understand your own emotions and react in a calmer way. That helps build stronger relationships.

A PROBLEM-BUSTING TOOL

Rating Your Emotions

You often feel a lot of different emotions each day. Some may feel intense, others less so. One way to better understand your emotions is to rate them, like this:

- When you feel an emotion, stop! Think about what emotion you are feeling. Are you excited, are you inspired, or are you upset? Name the emotion.
- Now, rate how strongly you feel that emotion on a scale of 1 to 10. Number 1 is the weakest emotion, one that'll pass in seconds, and 10 is the most intense of the emotions.
- If you score more than 5 for any emotion, talk to someone about it.

Instead of flying off the handle, when you're really upset, count to ten, and breathe. Think about how you feel and what you can change.

STUDIES IN TEEN SURVIVAL

The amygdala is the part of your brain that helps you handle intense emotions. The amygdala and your limbic system figure out if something is a threat and how to respond to it. Research shows that when you put your feelings into words, the amygdala responds differently. You then feel less emotional if and when the same thing happens again.

WHY SOCIAL AWARENESS WORKS

Learning about emotions is the first step toward being socially aware. Let's take another look at why being emotionally aware is important.

1 There Are No Right or Wrong Emotions

Every emotion you feel is valid but how you react to them makes a difference to your emotional wellbeing and that of others.

2 Emotional Awareness of Others Leads to More Empathy

We cannot be empathetic if we don't try to understand what others are feeling.

3 Telling Others How You Feel Is Good for You

When you talk to others about your emotions, you'll feel better. Keeping intense feelings to yourself can lead to anxiety and depression.

4 Identifying Emotions Helps Train Your Brain

When you can label an emotion, you can train your brain to react in a less extreme way if a similar situation arises. This will then reduce the stress of a negative emotional reaction.

Learn from the Past

If you experience extreme or intense emotions, both positive and negative, think about what triggered the emotions. What made you feel like that? If the trigger led to a positive emotional response, try to build more of that into your life. If you had a negative response, try to avoid the trigger in the future. Although this may not always be entirely possible, simply being aware of the trigger will help you respond better. Focusing on positive emotions and being aware of the negative triggers leads to better mental health and emotional wellbeing.

CHAPTER 2

You and Your Family: A Survival Guide

You may live with both your parents and a sibling, while your friend lives with just one parent and no siblings. Another friend may live with a parent and stepparent as well as half- or stepsiblings. Sometimes, extended families that include grandparents live together in one home. Families come in all shapes and sizes, and a family is considered the smallest unit of society.

Learning on the Job

When you live with other people, you naturally learn a lot from them. And you may not even be aware that you're learning. For example, by helping your mom or dad in the kitchen to prepare a meal, you may feel like you're just doing a chore. However, you are also learning how to cook so that one day, you will be able to do this independently. Just as you learn important life skills, social-awareness skills are first developed in families throughout childhood. You may not realize it, but simple actions such as taking turns to do something and sharing toys are the beginning of learning social skills.

As you grow older, you learn to put needs of others first. That might include caring for your younger siblings and helping older grandparents.

Your physical appearance, such as hair and eye color, is inherited from your parents. While you don't inherit behavior from parents, you do learn many ways to behave from them.

Getting It Right

Sometimes, when a teen tries to gain independence it can make life a little difficult. Your parents may not appreciate you trying to strike out on your own, and you may not want to listen to their thoughts and advice. Sooner or later, there is likely to be conflict and your family life may become a little more turbulent. To keep the peace at home and create a positive environment, you need to put some effort into mastering two important social-awareness skills. They are the skills of considering perspectives and cooperation. Master these two skills at home first and they will help you when you step into the wider world.

STUDIES IN TEEN SURVIVAL

As you become more independent, you may not always want to spend a great deal of time with your family. However, studies have shown that when people spend time together as a family, they are less likely to suffer from depression, anxiety, and other mental illnesses. The studies show that being with loved ones creates a strong emotional support that carries family members through difficult times.

In a group of friends, everyone will have their own perspective. By considering the perspectives of others, your friendships will be much healthier.

A Different Perspective

Your perspective is the way you think about and understand something. Perspective can also be considered your personal point of view, and it shapes how you act and react in many different situations.

Let's Talk about Considering Perspectives

Perspective is not just a random way of thinking or feeling about something. Rather, it's based on your life experiences, values, culture, and state of mind, among other things. Your perspective is also based on how your brain functions. Interestingly, your brain is wired to make YOU the very center of your world. You believe that you are the most important person and so, your opinions and experiences drive your decisions and perspective. Because of this, someone with a similar background may have a very different point of view. Either way, there is no right or wrong perspective. But we need to learn to consider other people's perspectives if we want to be more socially aware.

Defining Social-Awareness Skills: Considering Perspectives

Considering perspectives is being able to understand a situation from the point of view, or perspective, of another person. It means you put aside your own thoughts and instead put yourself in someone else's position. Although it's impossible to completely take the perspective of another person, the aim is to consciously try to do so.

THE SOCIAL-AWARENESS WORKSHOP

Not Considering Others

Not caring about the perspective of other people does not help in social situations. It can lead to conflict and resentment, as this example shows.

Imagine you and your friends usually go to the mall after school on a Friday. One afternoon, you notice some other teenagers nearby. You don't know them, but one of them waves you over. They introduce themselves, you get along, and they ask if you want to go to the movies tomorrow. You are really excited. You go home and immediately ask your dad if that is OK. But your dad is not happy. He doesn't know the teen, and says neither do you—he says you can't go. You yell, "That's so unfair! Don't you trust me?" Then you storm off to your room and slam the door.

You felt really angry—and you didn't think what you asked for was a big deal. But refusing to consider your dad's perspective did not help the situation. If you had shown a little more consideration, the situation could have been resolved. Let's take a look overleaf.

THE SOCIAL-AWARENESS WORKSHOP

Same situation, but with consideration.

Considering Other Perspectives

When you ask your dad if you can go to the movies with the teen from the mall, he is not happy. He doesn't know your new friend, and says neither do you. He says you can't go.

You feel upset, and go to your room to calm down. You think about your dad's point of view. You know he is right. You realize that it's not that he doesn't trust you. He is just trying to keep you safe. You speak to your dad again, and tell him how you feel. You agree that you will get to know your new friend better before making plans to go out. You and your dad are good again.

What Works Better Here?:

- You put yourself in your dad's shoes.
- You realize he is looking out for you.
- You keep calm, talk things through, and agree to a compromise that works.
- You both feel respected and understood.

Considering Perspectives —What Can It Do for You?

When you try to understand other viewpoints, you put yourself in other people's shoes. You can then keep calm and talk things through. Considering other people's perspectives shows that you respect them. They are then more likely to work with you to find solutions.

There's no need to shout at your parents! You'll have more success in putting across your argument if you explain your perspective clearly and calmly instead.

A PROBLEM-BUSTING TOOL

Practice Consideration

Considering someone else's perspective doesn't always come naturally. In fact, it takes a lot of practice. To work on this skill, follow these four steps:

- Write down your thoughts, feelings, and intentions.
- Now consider the other person's thoughts, feelings, and intentions. Write them down too.
- Think about whether your behavior should change based on the other person's thoughts, feelings, and intentions.
- Next, make the changes or explain your point of view clearly and calmly to the person.

Showing Respect

A big part of considering someone else's perspective, even if it's very different from yours, is showing that person and their perspective respect. Like many skills, respect doesn't always come naturally, but with practice, it will be easier. There are many benefits to being in a respectful relationship. Respect in a relationship builds feelings of trust, safety, and wellbeing. Because we get a lot of our self-worth from how we are perceived by people who care about us, feeling disrespected can lead to feelings of worthlessness.

When people don't feel respected, they don't feel good about themselves. Low self-worth can cause anxiety and depression.

The Answer Is in Your Gut

One of the biggest signs of a respectful relationship is in how you feel in your gut. Ask yourself, do you feel safe being around the person? When there's mutual respect—each person respecting the other—the answer is yes. You can both express yourselves and your perspective without fear or shame. And there's no yelling or talking over each other. You won't always agree with everyone but if there's respect, when you disagree, you listen to each other and are patient with each other. You can talk about your needs and wants. In a respectful relationship, both people are able to admit when they've made a mistake.

Teen Need to Know

If you are in a disrespectful relationship and feel unsafe, it's really important to talk to a trusted adult about this. Trusted adults include parents, older relatives, teachers, and counselors. And if you have a friend in a disrespectful relationship, try to encourage them to seek help too.

Recognizing Disrespect

Unfortunately, not all relationships are mutually respectful. Knowing what a disrespectful relationship looks like can help you navigate difficult relationships. Signs of a disrespectful relationship include:

- Being ignored, "ghosted," or given the silent treatment when you have a different perspective from the person
- Being criticized or insulted when you disagree
- Feeling humiliated, punished, blamed, or threatened
- Your thoughts and feelings are dismissed or minimized by the person
- Feeling that the things you say or your point of view is always wrong.

A PROBLEM-BUSTING TOOL

Dealing with Disrespect

You can't make someone respect you, but you can certainly try. One way to do this is to set boundaries. This means you tell someone how you feel and what doesn't work for you. You let the other person know that what they're doing isn't OK—be specific so that it's clear. Stand up for yourself with good, clear communication—you can learn more about this on pages 30–31.

Mutual respect is key to a healthy relationship.

Let's Talk about Cooperation

When you think about your own family, you'll soon realize just how different each family member is. Aside from your physical differences and the differences in age, you are probably not the same when it comes to your personalities. You could be shy and quiet while your sibling is loud and extroverted. Perhaps one of you is better at something than the other. These differences are a good thing but they also mean that everyone in the family has different needs, wants, and ideas. A parent will have different needs and wants from a young child, and a young child has different ideas from a teenager.

It's easy for everyone to want their own way and to put themselves first, but that doesn't necessarily work. Instead, it usually creates strife in the family. In order to avoid conflict, there needs to be cooperation between all members of a family unit.

When your parents ask you to do chores, it helps them and frees up some of their time. And if they have more free time, you'll be able to do more fun things together.

Defining Social-Awareness Skills: Cooperation

Cooperation in a family means that each person can balance their own needs, wants, and ideas with those of other family members. It means everyone works within a family to achieve their individual goals. And to do that, the family needs to pull together. This can mean helping each other with schoolwork, playing to individual strengths, or practicing sport together. It could also be giving kind advice to younger family when they need it.

Stop, Cooperate, and Listen

The first step to better cooperation in a family is for family members to understand each other's goals. Listen to what people are saying. What is each person aiming for? How can you pull together to help them achieve this? Each person in your family must be respected and valued, even if their goals are different from yours. For example, you may be really musical, while your sister is sporty. While you may want the lead in a school play, she'll want to be the best athlete. You don't have to take up running to show that you understand your sister but you can encourage her and support her at school meets. And she can support you by asking about your auditions and rehearsals.

Show your siblings that you care about their goals by supporting them at events.

STUDIES IN TEEN SURVIVAL

There are many benefits of cooperation (and they're all on the next page). Studies have shown that cooperative attitudes are better for people's mental health. Those who are cooperative are more open in their communication with others and have a far greater sense of belonging. This gives them a sense of security and wellbeing.

When families do things together, they bond.

The Benefits Are High

Cooperation is one of those skills that every family member benefits from. You may not see the benefits right now, but in time, you will. Some of the benefits of cooperation include bonding, building trust, belonging, and building a sense of confidence.

A Bonding Experience

One of the biggest benefits of cooperation in a family is bonding or coming closer together. Sometimes, you may feel that your younger siblings are irritating, and you might not want to be around them much. But remember, being part of a close family is a good thing. It means that there is always someone there for you, and someone to talk to who has a lot of the same shared experiences. In a close family, people care about each other, support one another, and want what's best for each other. This closeness means people feel that they are able to talk more openly and discuss their goals and ideas. The more a family talks and shares their feelings, the greater the cooperation.

Building a Team

When there is cooperation in a family, there's an innate trust between family members. Trust is important because it means that each family member knows that the others have their best interests at heart. This leads to people feeling secure and confident. Another benefit of cooperation is that because everyone is involved, decision-making becomes shared between family members. That helps create a feeling of being part of a team. Because there's shared responsibility, each person in the family is accountable to the others. Being accountable means that you take ownership of the consequences of your actions—you understand how they affect not just you, but your family too.

Building Self-Worth

It's a great feeling when you're part of a team and your team does well. If you feel like you are part of a winning team, it gives you a sense of high self-worth. If you have high self-worth, you will feel worthy of care, support, and compassion. Research shows that teenagers who have a high self-worth become confident adults.

Teen Need to Know

If you learn to cooperate at a young age, you'll feel more confident and comfortable doing so when you're older. You'll also be better able to assess when being uncooperative is necessary. Being uncooperative doesn't mean that you refuse to put the dishes in the dishwasher—it means that you consider why cooperating in the situation will not work for you. For example, perhaps your friend is asking you to share a cigarette or vape and you don't feel comfortable doing so, or perhaps you've been asked to lie about something and this goes against your values. You may find yourself in a situation in which a friend asks you to take their side in an argument with a shared friend, but you really don't want to and would rather not get involved in their conflict.

In situations that have negative consequences, you can be uncooperative and politely and respectfully say no. It helps to trust your gut feeling in these situations: If something doesn't feel right, have the confidence to be uncooperative.

WHY SOCIAL AWARENESS WORKS

Learning to be socially aware is complex and affects everyone in a family. This chapter has looked at two skills to help develop social awareness: considering perspectives and cooperation. Let's recap them.

1 Considering Perspectives Leads to Mutual Respect

When you show others that you respect them and understand their point of view, they are more likely to respect you, too.

2 Considering Perspectives Helps Others Feel Listened To

It's not always easy to understand another person's perspective but if you show that you're trying to, you will leave the person feeling listened to and valued.

3 Cooperation Is Key to Achieving Goals

If you know people who can help and encourage you to achieve your goals, your goals will be more attainable.

4 Cooperation Leads to Improved Wellbeing

When there is cooperation in families, members feel closer to each other, trusted, and valued. Teenagers who are able to cooperate become more confident adults.

Be a Little More Assertive

Assertiveness is a skill that allows you to express yourself and your opinions with confidence. But being assertive does not mean being aggressive if you feel someone is not understanding your point of view. Nor should you react aggressively if you feel they are expecting you to cooperate without considering what you want. Instead of shouting at the person, think about what they are saying and listen carefully to them. Then be prepared to say how you feel in a calm and respectful way.

CHAPTER 3

School, College, and Work

By the time you get into bed at night, you're likely pretty tired. That's because as a teenager, your days are incredibly busy. You're up early to go to school. You spend hours in class and later, taking part in sports or cultural activities. You probably haven't given it a lot of thought, but throughout your day, you encounter many different social situations. These can include working on group assignments with classmates. You might be on a team or in a band. Even just getting the bus home from school with other students means you need to mix socially.

These different social situations can feel overwhelming. However, once you master some social-awareness skills, managing school life will feel a lot easier. And you can then take these skills with you to college, and later, to work.

Social Awareness at School

You may be wondering why it's important to learn some specific social-awareness skills to help you during your school day. Well, when students develop social-awareness skills, they feel a sense of belonging and are better connected to their school. This helps them care more about how they perform at school because they feel a sense of pride in their

By working on your social-awareness skills, you'll be better equipped to handle busy days at school.

Some schools have programs that help students build their social-awareness skills.

performance and want to give it their all. School becomes a happy place, and one they like going to. However, on the flipside, if a teenager struggles socially at school and doesn't connect easily with their peers, school can become a place of anxiety and stress. And when teens feel stressed, they are less likely to perform as well as happier students.

Learning Powerful Skills

We've made a great start in learning social-awareness skills. However, what are the three new social-awareness skills that teenagers need to really thrive at school and beyond? The skills most beneficial to students are effective communication, understanding social signals, and identifying strengths and weaknesses in others.

STUDIES IN TEEN SURVIVAL

Many schools offer specific social-awareness programs as part of their curriculum. Known as Social Emotional Learning (SEL), students are taught the skills needed to cope in different social situations. A recent study looked at teenagers who participated in SEL programs at school to see if they are beneficial. And you probably won't be surprised by what the study discovered. The students who participated in SEL programs had better social skills, and far fewer behavioral problems. They also performed better academically than their peers. The study also found that students who received SEL instruction were more likely to graduate high school and study further after school.

Let's Talk about Effective Communication

To communicate means to share information. A person can communicate by speaking and listening. Together, speaking and listening are known as oral communication. People also write things down to communicate. Both of these forms of communication rely on people choosing the right words, and so are both types of verbal communication. What you say or write can have a lasting impact on someone, and in turn, on you. It's crucial that as a teenager, you learn to communicate effectively.

Brush up on your listening and speaking skills to communicate effectively.

Defining Social-Awareness Skills: Effective Communication

Effective communication enables people to do more than just share information. It allows them to build relationships, collaborate, and be empathetic. Instead of just connecting with each other, they are also making meaningful connections that help everyone feel heard and valued.

STUDIES IN TEEN SURVIVAL

In a 2023 report it was found that 72 percent of business leaders believe that effective communication had increased their team's productivity, and more than half of the workers who also were interviewed agreed.

Giving someone your full attention while they're talking shows that you're listening effectively.

Speaking and Listening

To communicate effectively you need to be able to speak AND listen. When you talk to someone, choose the right volume—if you're next to them, you don't need to raise your voice! If you do, they may feel that you're yelling at them, even if you aren't. Be confident and talk at a pace people can understand. If all your words blend into one, no one will understand you or want to listen to you.

Now the hard part: Think before you speak and choose your words carefully. Remember, everyone has their own thoughts and ideas. Be respectful and courteous. When it comes to listening, try to look the part. Show that you're listening by sitting or standing still. Don't be distracted by your phone or someone else who is having what seems to be a more interesting conversation in the next group of friends. Don't fiddle with things, because that sends the signal that you're not actually interested. When someone talks, make eye contact with them, and respond appropriately. And avoid interrupting—it shows others that you're no longer listening.

It's Effective Because...

Effective communication does more than just get the message across. It builds trust and fosters healthy relationships. When people can talk openly and feel like they've been listened to, it develops mutual understanding between people. If you show that you can communicate effectively, people are more likely to stop and believe what you are saying. Effective communication creates a positive space in which people feel respected and listened to.

STUDIES IN TEEN SURVIVAL

Today's teenagers are the only age group to have known social media and smartphones from an early age. Social media is a huge part of a teen's life. When questioned, 64 percent of teenagers said that they would rather eat the same food for the rest of their lives than be without social media! That's why it is so important to understand and manage its pitfalls.

Social media can be positive and negative. It's important to recognize that when using it.

Write It Down

Today, you can send messages instantly across the globe as long as you have an Internet connection. Email programs and apps such as WhatsApp, iMessage, Snapchat, as well as X, and other social media platforms have changed not just what we use to communicate, but also how we communicate.

The Positives

Thanks to the Internet, it's much easier to keep in contact with others, especially those who are far away. We can email or send messages, writing down things quickly, and relay the information quicker than ever before. Social media also gives a voice to those who may not have had a platform to share their thoughts and ideas.

The Negatives

There are also some disadvantages to online communication. Often, our phones ping with messages while we are doing other tasks. This interruption is known as digital distraction. Digital distraction makes it difficult to stay entirely focused. And when you're writing down messages, there is a potential for miscommunication: You have to guess how the person is feeling and read emotions into the message. Online communication also makes it easier for bullies and trolls to target people.

Online Communication Made Simple

So how do you make sure you communicate effectively online? Follow these simple guidelines:

- Think twice before you send a message or post something online.
- You won't be able to see or hear a person's reaction when you post, so think about their perspective first.
- Be specific so that what you write is not misinterpreted.
- Be respectful and kind (more about this later).
- If you wouldn't say something to a person's face, don't put it online.
- If you're on a group chat and don't agree with what is being said, say so and/or leave the group.
- If you or someone you know is being cyberbullied (more about this on page 53), report it to a trusted adult.
- Don't post things, especially personal photos, that you may later regret.

It's easy for people to hide behind a fake social media profile and say negative things. What you can't say in person, don't say online.

Let's Talk about Reading Social Cues

Now we know about effective verbal communication, what about the nonverbal clues that we add to our conversations to convey meaning? For example, when people roll their eyes, what are they really saying? Sometimes, people wink when they're saying something or use a sarcastic tone of voice. Would you take what they're saying literally or would you realize there is a hidden meaning to their words?

Defining Social-Awareness Skills: Reading Social Cues

Nonverbal clues such as facial expressions, body language, and how you use your voice are called social cues. Social cues are the signals people send to others to communicate without using words. Reading these signals means being alert to nonverbal communication and understanding what someone is saying, without them actually saying it.

Reading People

Facial expressions are the faces you pull when you're talking or listening. They tell others what you're feeling. Sometimes, you may not even realize that you're pulling a certain face. Your face just does it! It can be difficult to hide an honest facial expression. Watching how people move their bodies is also a great way to read people. Strong emotion affects your posture, or how you hold your body, and your gestures. The way your body shows your thoughts and emotions is called body language. When someone talks, always try to look at their body language.

Rolling your eyes when someone is talking is rude. It shows that you're bored or annoyed.

THE SOCIAL-AWARENESS WORKSHOP

Not Reading Social Cues

Let's take a look at what happens when people don't read the social cues effectively. Imagine you have a history class. Your teacher has given the class an assignment, and students are given partners to complete the work with. The project involves research, then presenting the findings. You are paired with a student you don't know well. They are pretty quiet. You go up to them and say, "Hey, we are working together." They look down, and mumble, "Yeah, OK, maybe." They frown and fidget with their fingers. That makes you feel annoyed. You have gone out of your way to talk to them. You think they are rude, so reply, "OK, suit yourself, but the assignment is due in two weeks' time."

THE SOCIAL-AWARENESS WORKSHOP

Same situation, but with noticing the cues.

Reading Social Cues

Your teacher has given the class an assignment, and you are paired with a student you don't know well. They are pretty quiet. You go up to them and say, "Hey, we are working together." They look down, and mumble, "Yeah, OK, maybe." They frown and fidget with their fingers. You feel a little annoyed, but notice the frown on their face. Then you spot that they are fidgeting with their fingers a lot. You think they look worried, so you say, "Don't worry, I think we'll do well. You can do the research and I love public speaking! We'll turn in a great assignment." The student looks relieved, and smiles, "Great, that sounds good."

What Works Better Here?:

- You see the student is frowning and fidgeting. You notice that they seem anxious. You read those social cues.
- You realize that they mumble because they aren't particularly confident. They look shy and worried, too.
- You build their confidence by saying you'll work well together.
- By taking on the job of public speaking, you relieve the pressure they feel and relieve some of their anxiety.

Reading Social Cues—What Can It Do for You?

By understanding that communication can be verbal and nonverbal, you will read social cues more effectively. By looking at someone's facial expressions and gestures, and listening to their tone of voice, you'll learn a lot more about what they are trying to say.

When you have to do group assignments, read the room and note how your teammates are feeling before you start the assignment. Taking time to do this will make everything easier in the long run.

A PROBLEM-BUSTING TOOL

Figuring Out Body Language

Body language gives away how someone really feels. Take a look at these cues to be more aware of your own body language and also that of others:

- **Arms crossed across chest:** The person is annoyed, closed off, angry, or stubborn.
- **Smiling:** The person is happy, warm, and friendly. Sometimes people smile when they're anxious or nervous, so you need to look for other cues that indicate this.
- **Tapping fingers:** People tend to do this when they're impatient or nervous.
- **Tilting their head to one side:** This is a sign of active listening. The person is listening intensely and is deeply interested in the conversation being held.
- **Standing up straight:** People who are confident stand up straight, while those who lack confidence often slouch or slump.
- **Looking down:** When people look down and don't make eye contact, it shows a lack of confidence or mistrust of the person they're talking to.
- **Twisting hair:** This is a sign of nervousness.
- **Biting bottom lip:** People bite their lips when they are nervous or not telling the truth.

Let's Talk about Identifying Strengths and Weaknesses in Others

It's a big wide world, and no two people in it are the same. Think about the teenagers in your class: There will be sporty teens, and more studious ones—and within that group there will be people who are great at math, and some who are better at languages. There are teens who are friendly and kind, ones who make people laugh without trying very hard, and also the teenagers who are organized and always seem to know exactly what's going on. Each and every person is good at something. And on the flipside, everyone could improve on something too.

Defining Social-Awareness Skills: Identifying Strengths and Weaknesses

A person's strengths include the unique traits, talents, and characteristics that make them successful. Their weaknesses are the things they need to work on—the things they may not be great at yet. Strengths and weaknesses are not the same for everyone, and there is no checklist that everyone should be working toward. Your strengths and weaknesses are unique to you. Everyone's strengths and weaknesses will vary depending on their abilities, skills, and experiences. Once you see that each person brings different strengths to society, you'll appreciate each person's unique value.

Everyone has strengths and weaknesses. Once you know what yours are, you'll be able to work on maintaining them and improving on them.

For a relationship to be healthy, your friends need to accept you and your weaknesses.

Proving Our Brains Wrong

Finding people's strengths can sometimes be harder than we anticipate. This is because our brains are wired to see what we don't like about people rather than their strengths. It's easier to find their weaknesses and to be critical of them. Being critical is not especially helpful though, is it? When you identify a person's weaknesses, you don't need to call them out. Instead, try to accept the person for who they are. When you accept someone, you often notice more of their strengths, and the weaknesses become less of an issue. And if you know someone struggles with something in particular, you can adjust your expectations and focus on their strengths.

Teen Need to Know

A person's strengths and weaknesses are not fixed. They can change with time and under different circumstances. Everyone needs to work on the things they are good at to maintain them. Working hard on your strengths and building on them promotes confidence. And when you're confident, others will naturally discover more of your strengths. As a teenager, it's easy to feel low about the things you're not good at. But remember, everyone has weaknesses and once you identify yours, you can use a positive mindset to see them as an opportunity for growth.

Why Social Awareness Works

You now have the tools to help you to be more socially aware at school, at college, and in the workplace. Let's recap what effective communication, reading social cues, and identifying strengths and weaknesses can do for you.

1 Effective Communication Builds Stronger Relationships

If you can get your point across, with respect and empathy, you will find your relationships improve.

2 Communication Requires Thought

You cannot erase what you say both in person and online. So think carefully before you say something, send that message, or post that comment.

3 Reading Social Cues Correctly Aids Understanding

By understanding not just the words, but the facial expressions, body language, and tone of voice, you will really understand what the person is "saying." This will help you react appropriately too.

4 Identifying Others' Strengths and Weaknesses Fosters Acceptance

We cannot change people but by understanding their strengths and weaknesses, it's easier to understand them.

Figuring It Out

It may seem strange to think about how you can use these social-awareness skills in the workplace, especially while you have years before you'll be part of the working world. But try to remember that these key skills don't just miraculously appear overnight. It takes time and patience to develop them, so start young and work on them. Even as an adult, you'll need to keep practicing. No one has perfect social-awareness skills!

CHAPTER 4

Friendships and the Wider World

Adolescence is a time of exploration and discovery. You're learning and discovering new things about yourself and the world around you all the time. You'll find out what you like and don't like independently of your parents. And you'll get to figure out your own set of ideas and values. It may sound like fun, getting to figure out who you are. But actually, it can be a lot to deal with—and it's even harder to deal with all of this on your own. One of the ways teenagers can cope with all this is by making lasting friendships. Through your friends, you'll be able to find your place in the wider world.

STUDIES IN TEEN SURVIVAL

A recent study explored how teenagers form friendships. It found that school is the main place to make friends: 87 percent of the teenagers interviewed said they have a close friend at their school. Thirty-five percent said that they have a close friend who lives far away, while 15 percent said they have a close friend whom they first met online.

Joining your local clubs is a good way to find friends who are similar to you.

Applying your social-awareness skills is a good way to make and keep friends.

Making Friends

Making friends is really important, but how do you find the right people when you are changing so much and may feel shy sometimes too? There are no hard-and-fast rules about making friends, but these tips may help:

- **Join a club:** Getting involved with teenagers who have the same interests as you is a good place to start.
- **Help others:** Volunteering in your community is a great way to meet people who live nearby.
- **Use body language:** Remember what you learned about body language in the previous chapter? Try to show that you're friendly and not aggressive—smiling always works!
- **Make an effort:** Don't wait for others to invite you, take a lead and invite them instead.
- **Choose well:** Surround yourself with people who make you feel good about yourself.

Apply Your Skills

Following the tips above will help you find and make good friends, but how do you keep those friendships? The key to being a good friend is to apply your social-awareness skills. Listen and communicate effectively with your friends, be respectful, and earn their trust. These are skills you now know all about. Then add some new skills. Being kind, resolving conflict, understanding diversity, and giving back are great tools to help you make and keep friends for life.

Let's Talk about Kindness

As you know, the daily life of a teen can be a bit of a roller coaster ride, filled with emotional ups and downs. The ups are great. But what about the not-so-good days? If you have a bad day, and your friend goes out of their way to make you feel better, your downward dip on the roller coaster is never as bad. Thanks to your friend's kindness, your day brightens and you feel better and less alone in the world.

A simple act of kindness will make everyone feel good about themselves.

Defining Social-Awareness Skills: Kindness

Kindness is more than being polite and friendly—although those qualities add to overall kindness. It's about treating those around you with care, compassion, concern, and acceptance. Being kind means you genuinely care about others and consider their wellbeing. When you realize someone is struggling, you can do something about this with an act of kindness. Sometimes, teenagers see kind people as pushovers. They may believe that in today's fast-paced world, kindness is a weakness. But this isn't true. It takes strength of character to be kind, especially in a difficult situation.

Why Be Kind?

When you're kind to someone, it's not just the recipient of your kindness who benefits. Amazingly, there are benefits for you too. It's proven that being kind creates a rush of endorphins. These are the chemicals in the brain that make us feel happy. That means when you are kind, the person you are being kind to feels great, but so do you too. Knowing that you've made someone happy will also give your confidence and self-worth a boost. When kindness is built into every day life, it reduces discrimination and inequality. The world becomes a happier, safer place.

A PROBLEM-BUSTING TOOL

The Kindness Challenge

Being kind doesn't always come easily and sometimes, we need a gentle reminder to be a little kinder to those around us. One way to do this is to look for opportunities to practice being kind. You can set up a kindness challenge for yourself (you can include your family members and friends in the challenge too). On a sheet of paper, draw up a calendar page for a month. (You can find blank calendar pages online to print, too.) Each day, try to do one act of kindness, and write it down on the calendar. Write down what you did and how it made you feel. At the end of the month, look back at your acts of kindness and ask yourself these questions:

- Did it become easier to be kind?
- How did being kind make you feel?
- How did you benefit?
- How did others benefit?

Looking after a neighbor's pet while they are away is a kind thing to do.

Let's Talk about Conflict Resolution

As a teenager, your new-found independence probably means that you have your own perspectives and preferences. However, these changes can lead to conflict with the people around you. A little bit of conflict is healthy and natural, but too much can be draining. And that's where conflict resolution comes in.

Defining Social-Awareness Skills: Conflict Resolution

Conflict resolution is the process in which people find a peaceful solution to a problem. There are several ways to solve a conflict, and no one fits all. Sometimes, a conflict is best solved by realizing you're not going to win the battle, giving up the argument, and moving on. Another way to solve a conflict is by reaching a compromise. A compromise means you weigh up the options and negotiate for a fair result. Other times, the conflict is too great for a person to deal with on their own and help is needed from another person. This is called third-party intervention.

If you feel that you aren't making any progress and need help with resolving a conflict, ask a trusted adult to step in.

Teen Need to Know

There are times when compromise is not the right way to deal with conflict. For example, if you're being bullied, you need third-party intervention immediately, calling on the help of a trusted adult. If you're in a situation where you feel threatened or uncomfortable, withdraw from the situation immediately and ask for help too.

THE SOCIAL-AWARENESS WORKSHOP

Unresolved Conflict

Let's take a look at what happens when conflicts are not resolved well. You and your best friend have a shared friend that you get along with really well. You often spend time together because you all play soccer and support the same team. You happen to live next door to the shared friend, and their family is friendly with your family. You've all got to know each other well, and you see a lot of each other on the weekends.

One weekend, you go to watch a game together—you, the shared friend, and both your families. You post a picture online of you and your friend at the game. Soon after, you get an angry message from your best friend. They are unhappy that they have not been included and were not invited to watch the game. You reply to their message, "It was a family thing, it's no big deal." But your friend is still not happy, and sends you another upset message. You ignore it. It's their problem after all.

When you see them at school the next week, they ignore you. It seems you aren't such great friends anymore...

Turn overleaf to see how conflict resolution would help in this situation.

THE SOCIAL-AWARENESS WORKSHOP

Same situation, but with conflict resolution.

Dealing with Conflict

You and your best friend have a shared friend. One weekend, you go to watch a game with that shared friend and your families. You post a picture of you and the friend online. Soon after, you get an angry message from your best friend. They are unhappy that they have not been included. You can see how it might look to them, so quickly reply, "I'm sorry I've upset you, but it was a family thing—here, look at this pic." And you take a photo of you all—family members included—then send it to your friend. "My mom says you are definitely invited to the next one too!" you add. Your friend messages back with a smiley face. They no longer feel left out, and the conflict has been smoothed over.

What Works Better Here?:

- You think about your friend's feelings before reacting—and you can see how things might look to them. You'd be upset too.
- You immediately respond with a message to explain the situation.
- The conflict is quickly resolved, and you all move on.

Conflict Resolution—What Can It Do for You?

When you have a problem with a friend, sibling, or parent, put your social-awareness skills into action. Try to understand what the other person is feeling, think about things from their perspective, and communicate effectively with them to resolve the issue.

A PROBLEM-BUSTING TOOL

Conflict Resolution

It's easy to fly into a rage, but it's always better to resolve the conflict without lashing out. Try to stay calm—take a deep breath and count to ten. When you're calm, you'll be able to think more clearly. If you're able to, resolve the conflict in person. Talk to them by putting your communication skills into practice and make eye contact, actively listening to the person. Try to not interrupt the person while they're giving their side of the story. Be honest and specific about how you feel. But make sure it's all about how you feel NOW—don't bring up the past. If you can't or don't want to reach a compromise, ask an adult for their help—they may need to intervene.

Try talking to your friend about how something makes you feel before you are so angry that you say something you will later regret.

STUDIES IN TEEN SURVIVAL

Research has shown that friendships are healthier when friendship circles are diverse. A diverse friendship circle means people bring different ideas and experiences to the group. Without realizing it, friends learn from one another. The diversity also helps people grow, remove biases, and get along with a lot of different people in the wider world.

Let's Talk about Diversity Awareness

There are around 8 billion people in the world today—that's a lot of people! And as you've learned, no two people are alike. People look different, they have different backgrounds and beliefs, and each person has their set of physical abilities. These differences in people are known as diversity.

Defining Social-Awareness Skills: Diversity Awareness

Young children are born without biases. However, as children grow up, they learn biases from their family, friends, peers, and the outside world. Sometimes, they may not even realize that they have them. To prevent biases, we need to learn the skill of diversity awareness. Diversity awareness is about recognizing, respecting, and valuing differences based on race, ethnicity, age, gender, religion, socio-economic status, and physical ability. Diversity can certainly drive people apart. However, when it's celebrated and people focus on the positive aspects of their differences, everyone benefits. Overleaf you'll learn more about the many benefits of diversity awareness.

When diversity is celebrated, the world is a more welcoming place.

You can learn a lot from friends who have different cultural backgrounds from your own.

It's a Diverse World

In today's world, there are many different types of diversity, and each type impacts a person's life in some way. The types of diversity include:

- **Race:** The color of a person's skin will affect how they experience life.
- **Ethnicity:** A person's culture and nationality, or ethnicity, will impact their perspective. For example, if your friend has parents who immigrated to the United States, they will see things differently from a child's parents who grew up in the United States. The same can even be said for people who come from different areas or regions within the same country.
- **Gender:** Men and women experience things differently.
- **Age:** Each generation lives through historic moments that shape how they see the world. Think about your grandparents, parents, millennials, Gen Z—each generation has a different story to tell about what they went through.
- **Religion:** There are many different religions. Even in your own friendship circle, there may be Christians, Muslims, or Jews, or people with different religions. Some people do not follow any religion, and this will frame their experiences and values too.
- **Socio-economic status:** This refers to a person's education, income, and occupation.
- **Physical ability:** An able-bodied person will see the world differently from a less-able-bodied person.

Everyone's a Winner

Being aware of diversity has many benefits, and not just for your teenage years. You'll be able to take these benefits with you throughout your life. When people recognize diversity, it helps everyone feel like they belong. When everyone has a seat at the table, they know their opinions and ideas matter. People feel comfortable and welcome in all situations, especially those that are different from their usual experiences.

Diversity awareness also builds sensitivity toward others, and this helps develop empathy (see page 53). Those who are part of a minority group of people will have an easier time if everyone is aware of their differences. Diversity-aware people are generally more open-minded and can learn from being around different people. They learn about new cultures and religions, and embrace this newfound knowledge. Together, and when put into practice, all these factors result in better mental health for everyone.

By having a diverse group of friends, you will be able to consider different perspectives more easily.

Kindness, Empathy, and Acceptance

Earlier in the book we looked at kindness in detail. We also learned that empathy is being able to consider other people's perspectives, and understand and feel their response to a situation. Kindness and empathy, along with acceptance, are key to diversity awareness. Acceptance of diversity means that a person is able to recognize and respect other people's differences. You don't just tolerate, or put up, with their differences, you accept the person for those differences. If you learn to be more accepting of other people as a teen, you'll become an adult who is fair, respectful, and embraces diversity.

There would be fewer bullies if people were more aware of diversity and its benefits.

Teen Need to Know

Not everyone is tolerant and accepting of others. Sometimes, people are bullied for being different. Bullying can be carried out in person or online. In person, bullying can be verbal. People use words to taunt and tease others. It can be psychological—the bully does things to make others feel bad about themselves. Physical bullying is any form of touching that is unwanted. It includes kicking, punching, and touching inappropriately. Cyberbullying or online bullying can include sending abusive texts and/or posting abusive comments. It can also be uploading personal photos of a person without them giving consent.

Bullying can lead to stress, anxiety, and depression. Being bullied may result in a person having problems eating and sleeping, and feeling lethargic. If you or someone you know is being bullied, talk to a trusted adult. And, if you realize that YOU are a bully, it's never too late to change. Try seeking help from a school counselor or another adult you feel you can talk to.

When people feel they are part of a community, they are happier and have a sense of belonging.

Let's Talk about Giving Back

We live in a world in which a lot happens online. We shop online, we chat to friends through the Internet, and we can even learn online. Because of this, there can be limited face-to-face interaction with our direct community. Not having contact with our neighbors and the people who live in our area can lead to feelings of isolation. It also makes people feel that they are not part of their community. In order to reconnect, we need to give back to our community.

Defining Social-Awareness Skills: Giving Back

When people hear the words "giving back," they automatically assume it's about giving money to a cause they feel is worthy. However, giving back is much more than that. To give back also means to spend your time, experience, skills, and talents to help improve your community. If you are not financially able to donate money, you can give of your time or expertise instead. For example, if you are good with animals, you could help at your local dog shelter. If you are good at reading, you could volunteer to read at a home for the elderly. Anyone can give back and by doing so, everyone in the community benefits.

Why Giving Back Is Good

Giving back enriches your community. A community in which people give of themselves becomes close knit. And as we discovered with families, when communities are close, there are many benefits. Many communities only thrive because people give back. In these communities, people who volunteer are given a sense of purpose by serving others. Teens who contribute to their communities and help others have improved moods, lower stress, and fewer health problems. They are happier and have improved self-esteem. They also learn to be generous, which is a powerful trait that they can take into their adult lives.

STUDIES IN TEEN SURVIVAL

According to a survey, many teenagers say they have become more aware of the needs of others as a result of using social media. The survey found that the age group with the highest percentage of volunteers was 16 to 17 year olds. In that age group, nearly one-third had volunteered with at least one organization.

Your time is valuable, so offering to give up some of it is a great way to give back to your community.

WHY SOCIAL AWARENESS WORKS

You now have some great skills to help steer you through being more socially aware. Let's revisit the skills of being kind, conflict resolution, diversity-awareness, and giving back to see their many benefits once more.

1 Being Kind Benefits Everyone

Trying to be kind will benefit both those around you and yourself. Those who are kind are less likely to struggle with depression and do better both academically and professionally.

2 There Are Different Ways to Resolve Conflicts

There's no need to yell and scream when things don't go your way. Take a deep breath, and listen carefully and respectfully to the other person. Then you can either agree, compromise, walk away, or ask for help to deal with the situation.

3 Diversity Awareness Develops Acceptance and Understanding

When you recognize and understand people's differences, you can accept them for who they are and understand their perspectives more clearly.

4

Giving Back Is Good for Everyone

It is not just the recipient who feels good when people give back. Giving back of your time, talent, experience, goods, and money leaves you feeling more connected to your community.

Remember to Keep Learning

Working on social-awareness skills is a lifelong process. No one gets it right all the time. People have slip-ups, and sometimes it can be really difficult to think of others before yourself. But don't give up. If each person practiced a little more social awareness, the world will be a more tolerant, happier place.

CONCLUSION

Skills for Life

Social-awareness skills are vital for you to be a part of your family, your school environment, to have friends, and to be active in your community. You need them to be a good citizen. Set yourself some goals on how you can use and improve on these new skills. You may find it easier to start with one skill at a time and work through that alone. When you feel confident with that skill, move on to the next one. And to set you on your way, here are some important guidelines to steer your course.

Don't Forget to Reflect

Self-reflection will help you keep a close track of your progress. For example, when you feel overwhelmed emotionally, go back to the first chapter and see how emotional awareness can help. Flick through the rest of the book for other tips to help you cope.

Engage with Others

Use effective communication and read the social cues to improve your skills in sharing how you think and feel with others. Remember to treat others with kindness and empathy too.

The key to happiness is to work on your social-awareness skills so that you become an expert in reading the room.

You first learn social-awareness skills as a child. Now you need to develop those skills so that you become an adult who is kind, respectful, and one who makes a difference in the world.

If in Doubt, Ask

If you are unsure how to manage a difficult social situation, ask a trusted adult to help you. Parents, teachers, and counselors are all there to help when the going gets tough. They have had years of practice working on their social-awareness skills. They will be able to help guide you through difficult times as a result.

Share Your Skills

Don't keep your newfound skills to yourself, either! Remember to share what you've learned with friends and family. You've got some great tools under your belt now, and are in a position to help others work on their social-awareness skills. And the more everyone is on board, the healthier all our communities will be.

Glossary

adolescence the time of life when someone goes through the process of changing from a child into an adult

anxious nervous or worried

ashamed a painful feeling of humiliation or distress caused by wrong or foolish behavior

benefits the advantages a person gains from something

biases preferences not based on fact or experiences

colleagues people who work with one another

compassion to recognize the suffering of others and to try to help them

confident describes a person who has a sense of security in their abilities, qualities, or ideas

conflict a disagreement or argument

consequences the results and effects of something

courteous polite and respectful

critical describes someone who expresses disapproving comments or judgments

curriculum what is expected to be taught in a specific class

depression a mental illness in which a person has a low mood and lack of interest in most activities

effectively working well

embrace to accept or believe in something

emotional distress a very unpleasant emotion reaction

fatigue extreme tiredness

generous describes a person who is very giving

gestures movements of the body, usually the hands or head, to express an idea or meaning

hormones chemicals in the body that help the organs function properly

humiliated made someone feel foolish or ashamed

identities the ways in which people perceive themselves

immigrated moved to one country from another

independent without needing any help

innate inbuilt and instinctive

intentions aims

lethargic sluggish and apathetic

limbic system the group of structures in the brain that regulate a person's emotions, behavior, motivation, and memory

miscommunication a failure in communication when someone misunderstands the communication

mood swings sudden changes in mood

mutually respectful when everyone is treated with respect

negotiate to discuss something in order to come to an agreement

nonverbal without words

occupation a job or profession

open-minded describes a person who is willing to consider new ideas

overwhelming too difficult to deal with

peers people who are roughly the same age

positive mindset keeping a frame of mind that looks for the positives rather than the negatives in every situation

preferences things a person likes or prefers

productivity how effective something is

random describes something done without method or order

recipient someone who is given something

reflect to think carefully about something that has happened

resentful feeling bitterness

self-confidence a person's belief in their abilities

self-worth a measure of whether a person feels good enough and worthy of love

sensitivity the ability to easily detect or respond to slight changes, signals, or influences

sibling a brother or sister

stepparent the person a divorced parent marries when they remarry

strife conflict and difficulty

tolerant allowing the opinions or behavior of a person, even if one does not agree with them

traits distinguishing qualities or characteristics

triggered made to feel a certain way

turbulent something that has conflict and disorder

turmoil disorder

valid reasonable and accepted as true

values morals and beliefs

Find Out More

BOOKS

Gladdin, Kate. *The Teen's Guide to Social Skills: Practical Advice for Building Empathy, Self-Esteem, and Confidence*. Callisto Teens, 2021.

Teen Thrive. *A Teen's Workbook for Conquering Social Anxiety: How to Navigate Social Situations, Develop Self-Esteem, and Manage Fear and Shyness*. Teen Thrive, 2024.

WEBSITES

For anything relating to teenage health and wellbeing, visit Go Ask Alice at:
https://goaskalice.columbia.edu/about-go-ask-alice

Visit the Positive Action website for useful information on social awareness at:
www.positiveaction.net/blog/social-awareness

ORGANIZATIONS

For more help with social-awareness skills, take a look at these two great organizations:

Teen Lifeline, PO Box 10745, Phoenix, AZ 85064
602 248 8337
Website: teenlifeline.org

Teen Line, 4760 S. Sepulveda Boulevard Culver City, CA 90230
800 852 8336
Website: www.teenline.org

Publisher's note to educators and parents:
All the websites featured above have been carefully reviewed to ensure that they are suitable for students. However, many websites change often, and we cannot guarantee that a site's future contents will continue to meet our high standards of educational value. Please be advised that students should be closely monitored whenever they access the Internet.

Index

About the Author

Jennifer Sanderson has written books on many different topics, from tennis and baby animals to geography and self-care. She has two teenagers who, like all young people, are learning to navigate life's ups and downs by becoming more independent. She's hoping this book will give them and other readers the skills they need to go from the roller coaster of being teenagers to fully-fledged socially-aware adults.